WHO WERE THE JACOBINS?

FRENCH REVOLUTION HISTORY BOOK FOR KIDS | CHILDREN'S EUROPEAN HISTORY

In France in 1789 and after, people struggled with great questions. Who should run the country? Should we have a king? The Jacobins started as a discussion group that became a powerful force in the French Revolution. Let's find out about them.

TURBULENT TIMES IN FRANCE

France, in the eighteenth century, was a weak country with a strong history. It had been a major power in European affairs since the empire of Charlemagne in the ninth century. However, the more recent rulers of France, both kings and the nobility, had not been effective.

The country was heavily in debt, had lost some major wars, and was experiencing a crippling division between rich and poor. A tiny number of wealthy people controlled almost all the money and power in France, and the great majority of people had lives of hard work and limited opportunity.

AMERICAN REVOLUTION

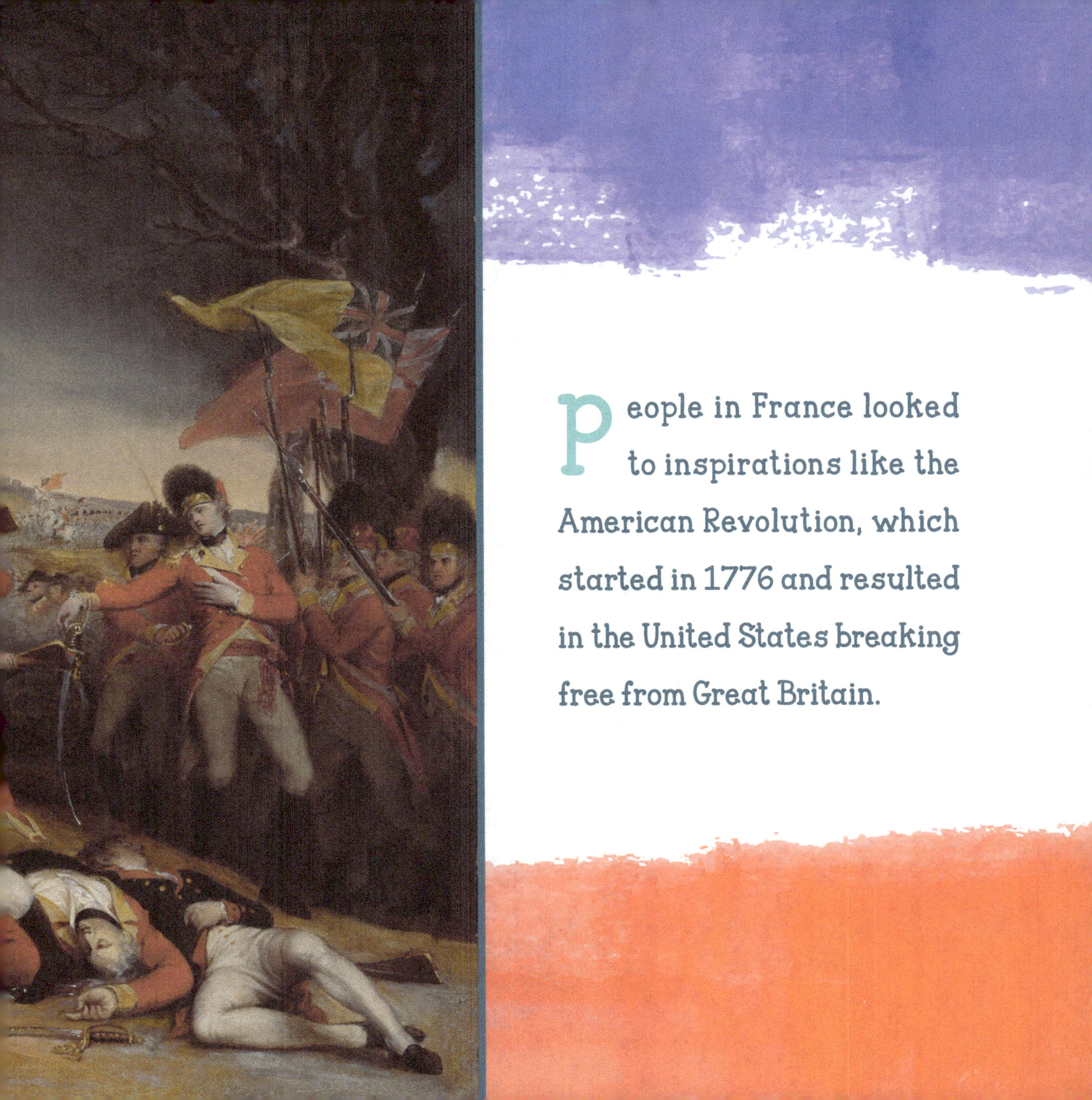

People in France looked to inspirations like the American Revolution, which started in 1776 and resulted in the United States breaking free from Great Britain.

People in France were inspired by that revolution's Declaration of Independence, which proclaimed that all people had the right to life, liberty, and the pursuit of happiness. Many in France felt that people would never be assured of those things if they continued to be governed by kings and a few wealthy families.

DECLARATION OF INDEPENDENCE

A Discussion Group Becomes a Power Group

In 1789, King Louis XVI convened the Estates General, a body that had to meet to approve new taxes. The last time it had met was in 1614! The rulers of France were afraid that if that group met, it might work on other things besides approving taxes, and might enact laws or make changes that the rich and powerful did not want. And that is exactly what happened.

KING LOUIS XVI

The Estates General created a new body, The National Assembly, to write a new constitution for France. Part of their plan was to limit the power of the king.

ESTATES GENERAL

RUE DE JACOB

Delegates to the Estates General, and then to the National Assembly, from Brittany started to meet regularly to discuss policy. They met at former monastery of the Dominican friars on the Rue de Jacob in Paris. The friars had become known as "Jacobins" because of the street their building was on, and the political group also became known by that name.

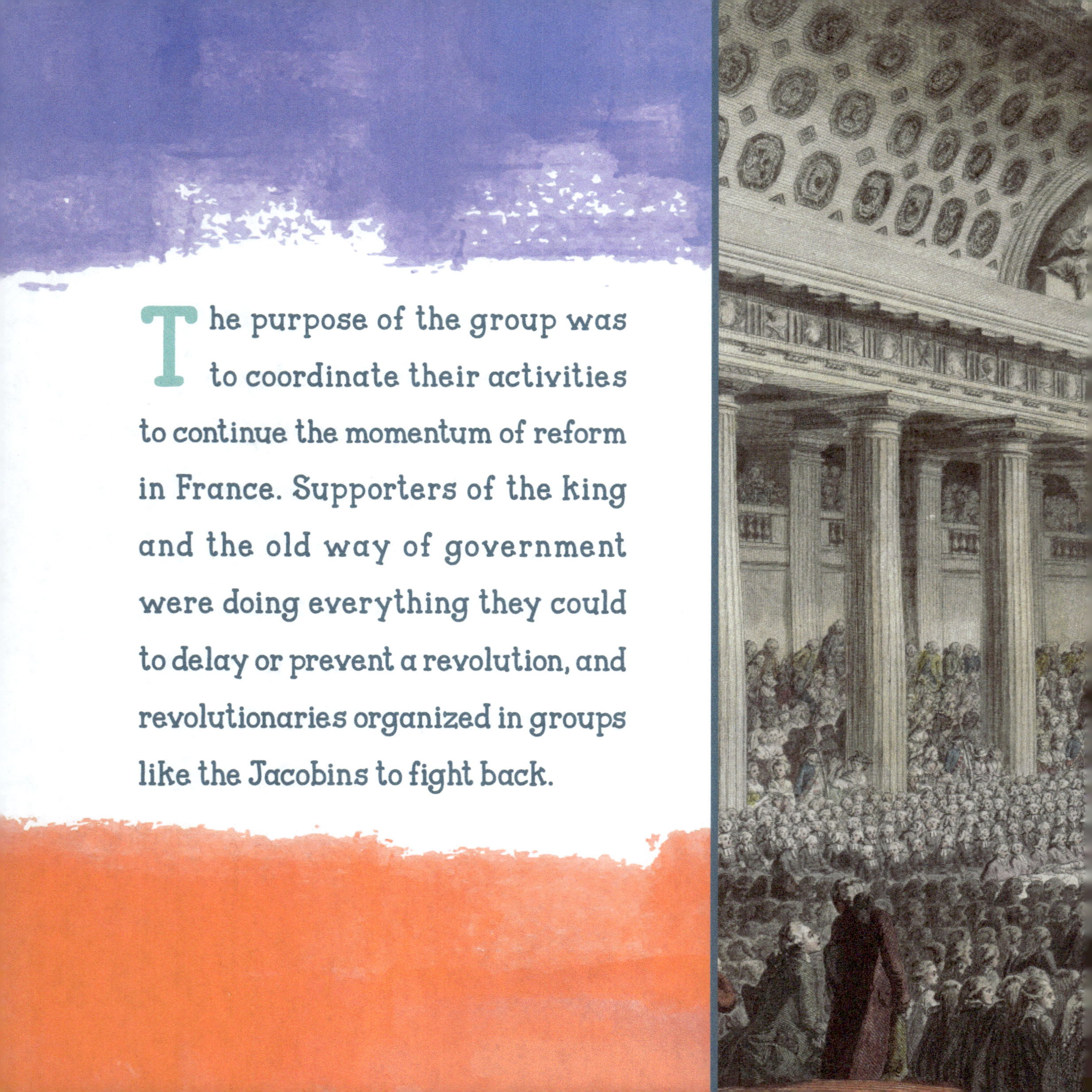

The purpose of the group was to coordinate their activities to continue the momentum of reform in France. Supporters of the king and the old way of government were doing everything they could to delay or prevent a revolution, and revolutionaries organized in groups like the Jacobins to fight back.

JACOBIN CLUB

The Jacobins had as many as 1,800 members in Paris, and founded clubs in other cities throughout France. About half a million men across France belonged to the clubs. Women were not allowed to be members, although they could attend the discussions and listen.

Within the National Assembly, the Jacobins coordinated their efforts to push for the policies and rules of government that they wanted put in place. While much of the anger and demand for change came from the working poor and the peasants,

most of the members of clubs like the Jacobins were from the educated middle class. They published their opinions in newspapers and pamphlets, and spoke about the need for change at public meetings.

The Jacobins wanted to limit the powers of the king, and put more power in the hands of an assembly of elected representatives. But some Jacobins wanted to see the monarchy continue in some sort of limited way, while others wanted to abolish it altogether. The most extreme members of the group wanted to see the king, the royal family, and the nobility executed for crimes against the people.

NATIONAL ASSEMBLY OF FRANCE

PRUSSIAN ARMY
bei Mollwitz.
April 1741.

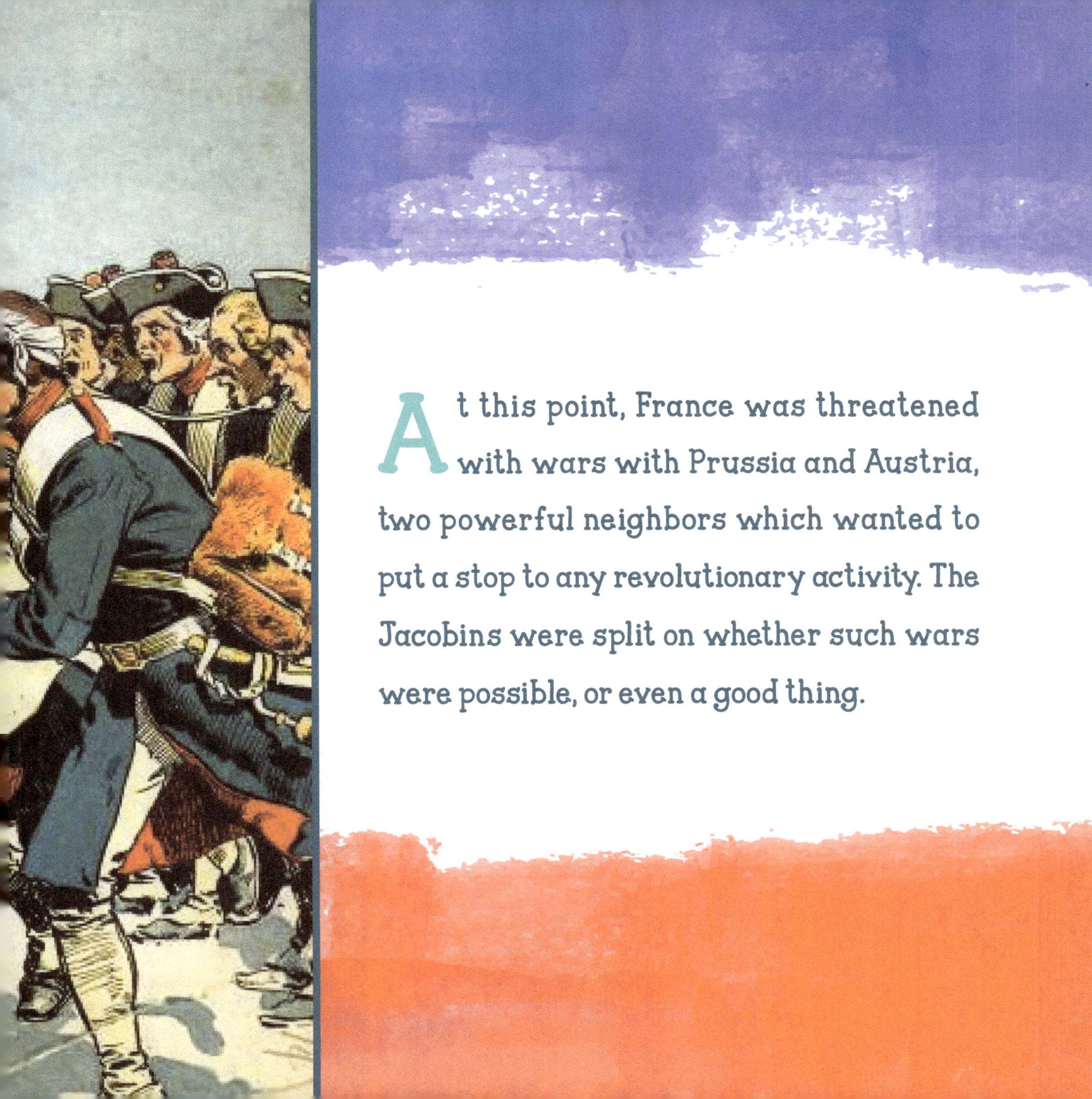

At this point, France was threatened with wars with Prussia and Austria, two powerful neighbors which wanted to put a stop to any revolutionary activity. The Jacobins were split on whether such wars were possible, or even a good thing.

As discussions continued, the Jacobins developed more and more radical positions, including:

- The government should be an elected assembly

- Every adult, male citizen should have the right to vote, not just the wealthy

CONVENT OF THE JACOBINS

CHURCH OF THE JACOBINS IN TOULOUSE

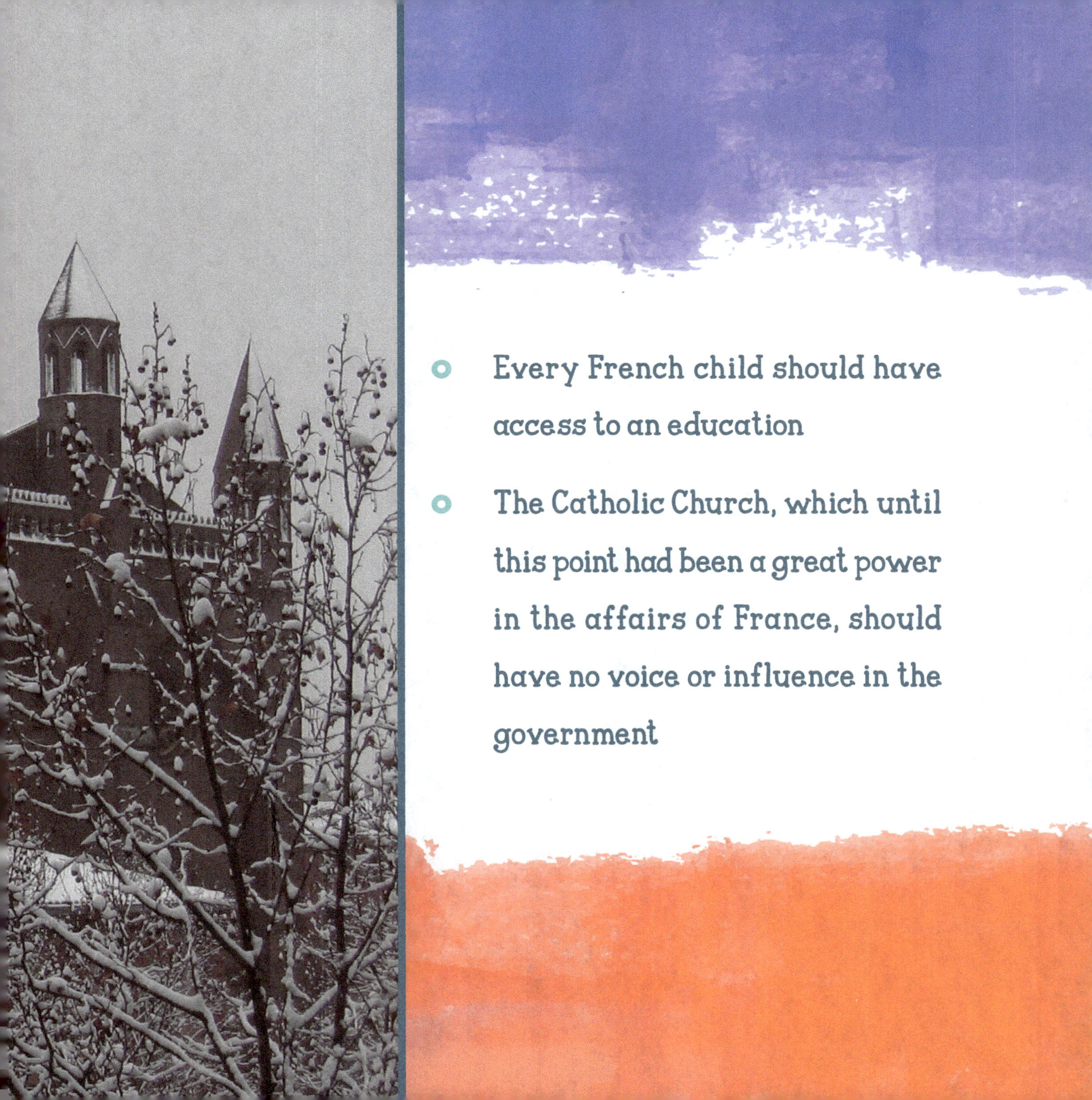

- Every French child should have access to an education

- The Catholic Church, which until this point had been a great power in the affairs of France, should have no voice or influence in the government

THE GIRONDISTS

Another major body in the Revolution was known as the Girondists. Many of their leaders came from the Gironde region of France, but the movement had powerful members throughout much of France. They were, however, much weaker in Paris than the Jacobins.

GIRONDIST COLUMN IN FRANCE

From the start of the revolution in 1789 until sometime in 1793 the Girondists had a stronger leadership position than the Jacobins did.

During this period, war started with both Austria and Prussia, King Louis XVI was removed from power, and the French Republic was created. But to the Jacobins, this was not enough change!

BATTLE BETWEEN AUSTRIA AND PRUSSIA

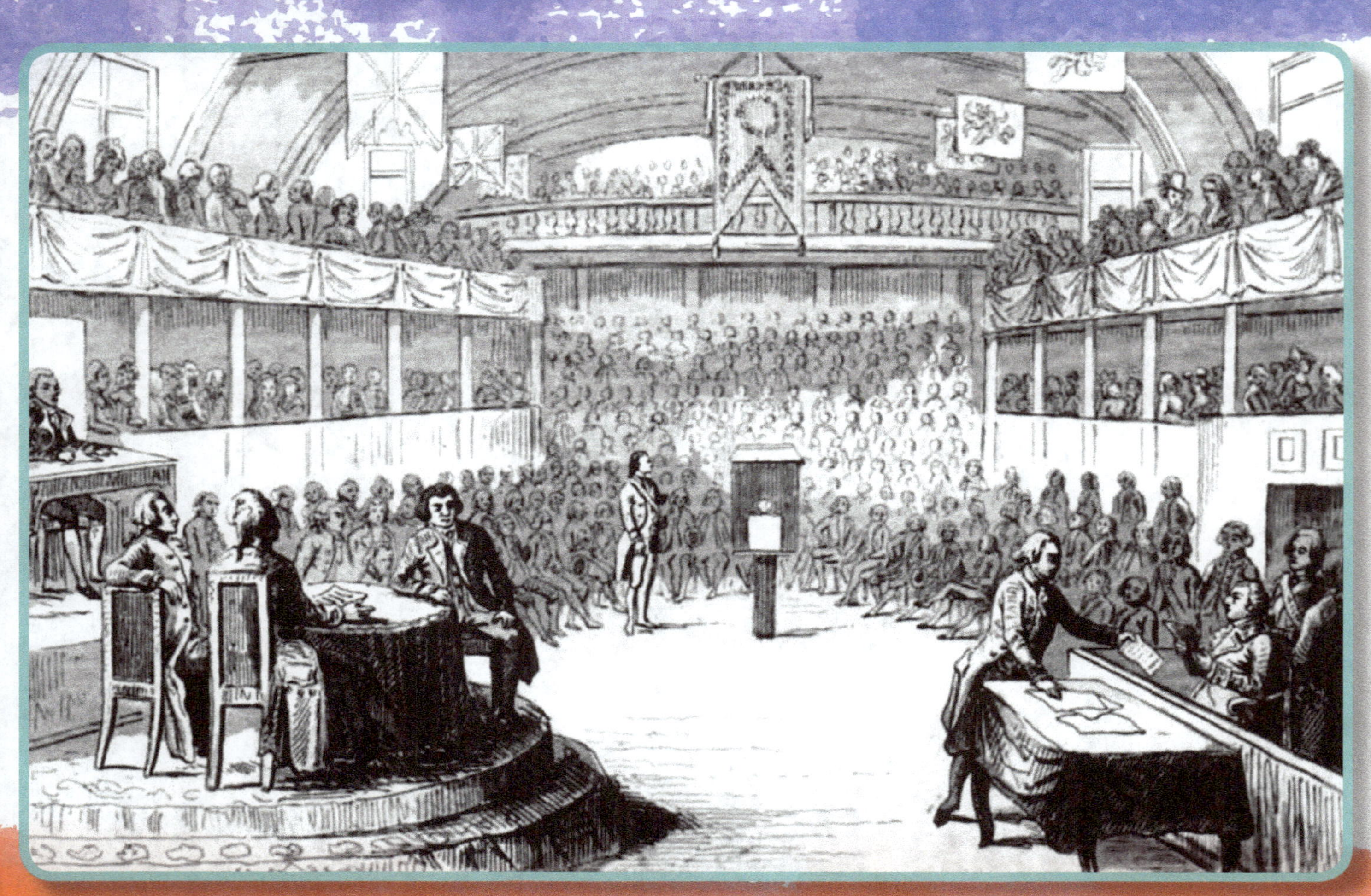

National Convention

IN THE NATIONAL CONVENTION

In the new National Convention, which started governing France in September, 1792, there were about 750 delegates from all over France. The Jacobins and their allies tended to sit in seats high up at one side of the assembly space, and they came to be known as "the mountain" from their high location in the room.

The Jacobins and their allies ("the mountain") had about 120 delegates, with Maximilien de Robespierre, a lawyer, as one of their most effective leaders; the Girondin group, who sat at the other extreme of the hall, had about 150. The remaining 470 or so delegates, seated in the middle and not formally allied with either group, were known as "the plain".

M any of these delegates found the Jacobin ideas far too radical, and were happy to support the Girondist members in election to leadership positions. It was members of "the plain" who mainly pushed ahead concrete measures and proposals for laws, while the Jacobins and Girondists got tangled up in arguments about obscure details and definitions of terms.

GIRONDIST COLUMN

SEIZING POWER

The Jacobins had a great ally: public opinion. They were seen by the peasants, the poor, and a militant group known as the sans-culottes (for the clothes peasants typically wore: a smock bound with a belt, and no long trousers), as bearing the true spirit of the revolution.

These groups became increasingly convinced that the Girondists, far from being revolutionary, were actually working to protect the rich and the nobility.

TUILERIES PALACE

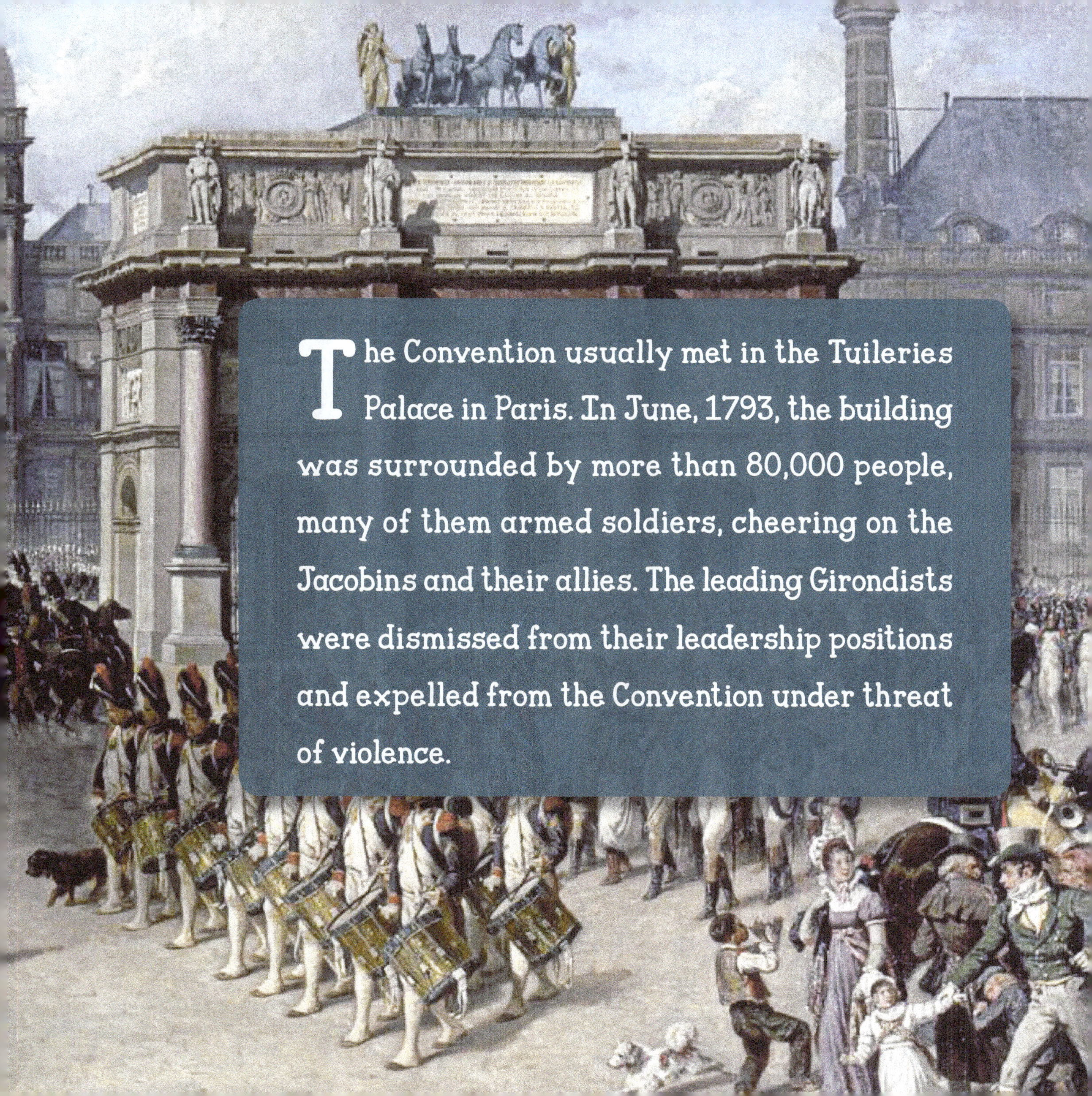
The Convention usually met in the Tuileries Palace in Paris. In June, 1793, the building was surrounded by more than 80,000 people, many of them armed soldiers, cheering on the Jacobins and their allies. The leading Girondists were dismissed from their leadership positions and expelled from the Convention under threat of violence.

A FORCE FOR TERROR

The Jacobins and their Mountain allies controlled the government from May, 1793 until July, 1794. During this period, France was dealing with wars with Austria and Germany, and rebellions against the revolution in many parts of France.

COLOGNE, FRANCE 1794

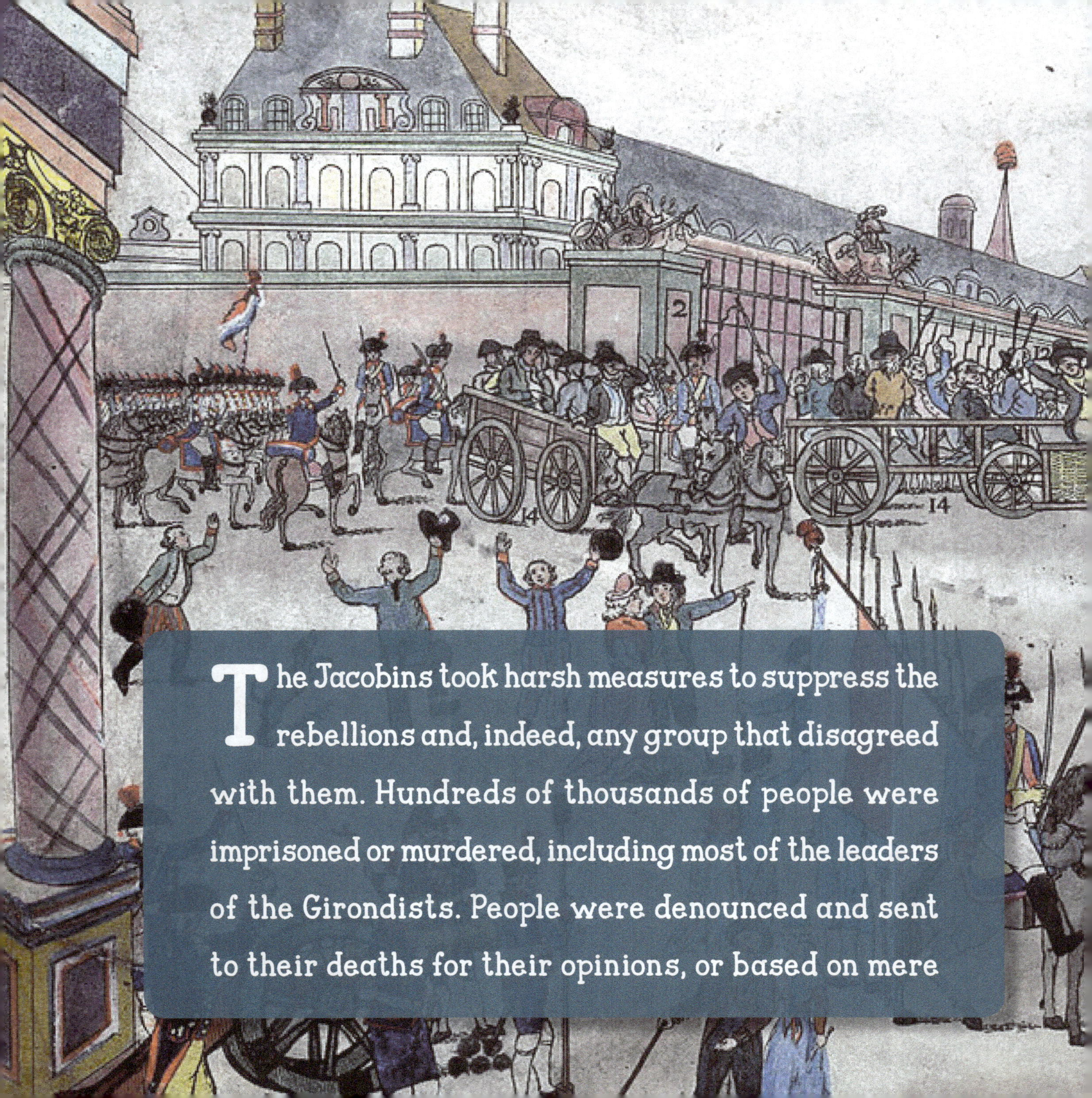

The Jacobins took harsh measures to suppress the rebellions and, indeed, any group that disagreed with them. Hundreds of thousands of people were imprisoned or murdered, including most of the leaders of the Girondists. People were denounced and sent to their deaths for their opinions, or based on mere

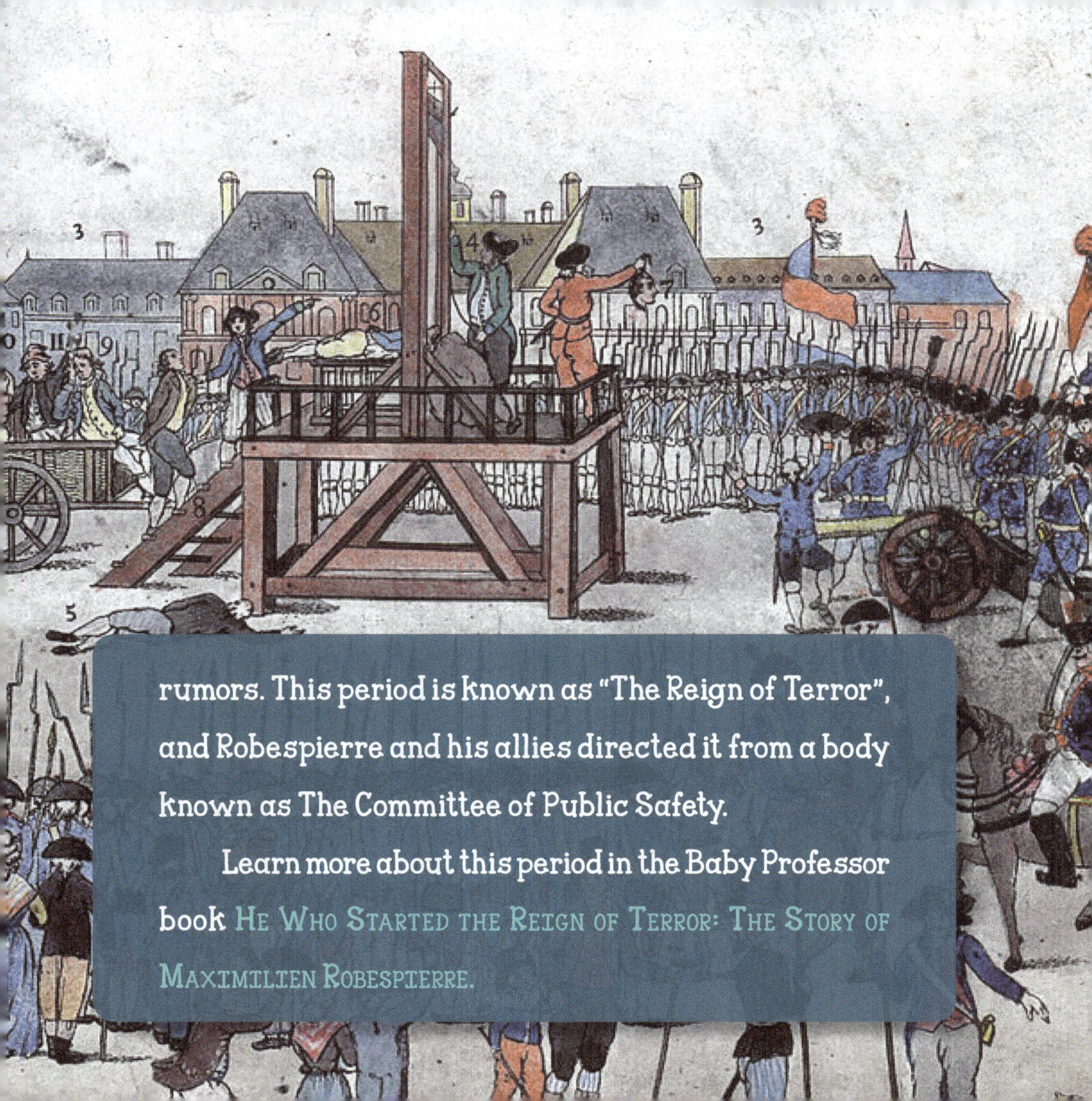

rumors. This period is known as "The Reign of Terror", and Robespierre and his allies directed it from a body known as The Committee of Public Safety.

Learn more about this period in the Baby Professor book HE WHO STARTED THE REIGN OF TERROR: THE STORY OF MAXIMILIEN ROBESPIERRE.

JACOBIN CLUB 1794

THE END OF THE JACOBINS

Finally, many in power felt the Jacobins, and Robespierre in particular, had gone too far. Some also felt that they might be the next to be arrested, and that they had better end the Reign of Terror or become its victims.

In July, 1794, the Jacobins were forced out of power. Robespierre and many of his allies were arrested. He and 21 associates were executed.

ARREST OF ROBESPIERRE

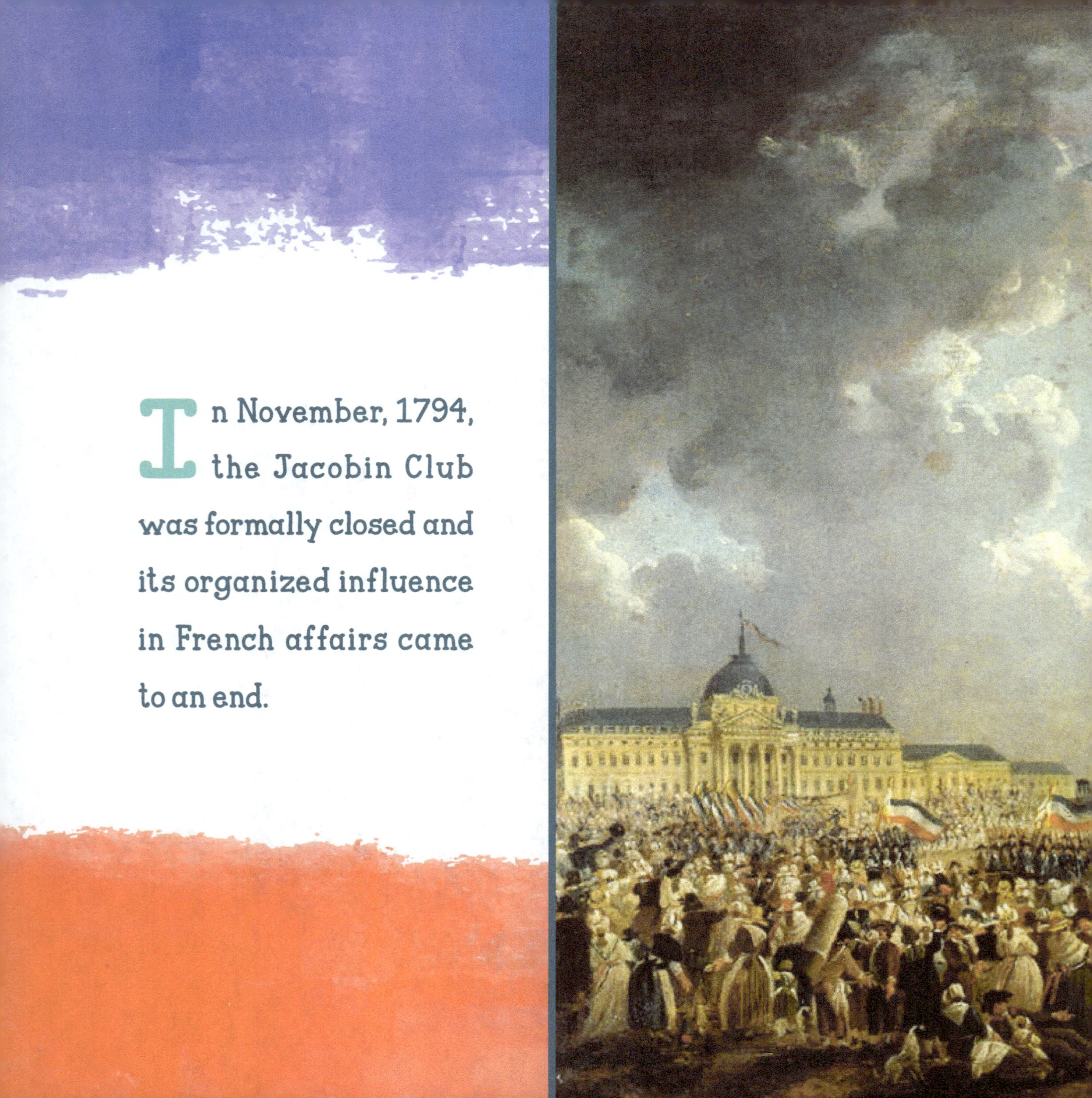

In November, 1794, the Jacobin Club was formally closed and its organized influence in French affairs came to an end.

THE FESTIVAL OF THE SUPREME BEING
ESTABLISHED BY ROBESPIERRE

THE NEXT STAGE

Both Jacobins and Girondists had exciting ideas for how France should be governed, but in practice neither party governed well. France was also crippled by the expenses of several wars at the same time and the effects of a drought that caused crop failures.

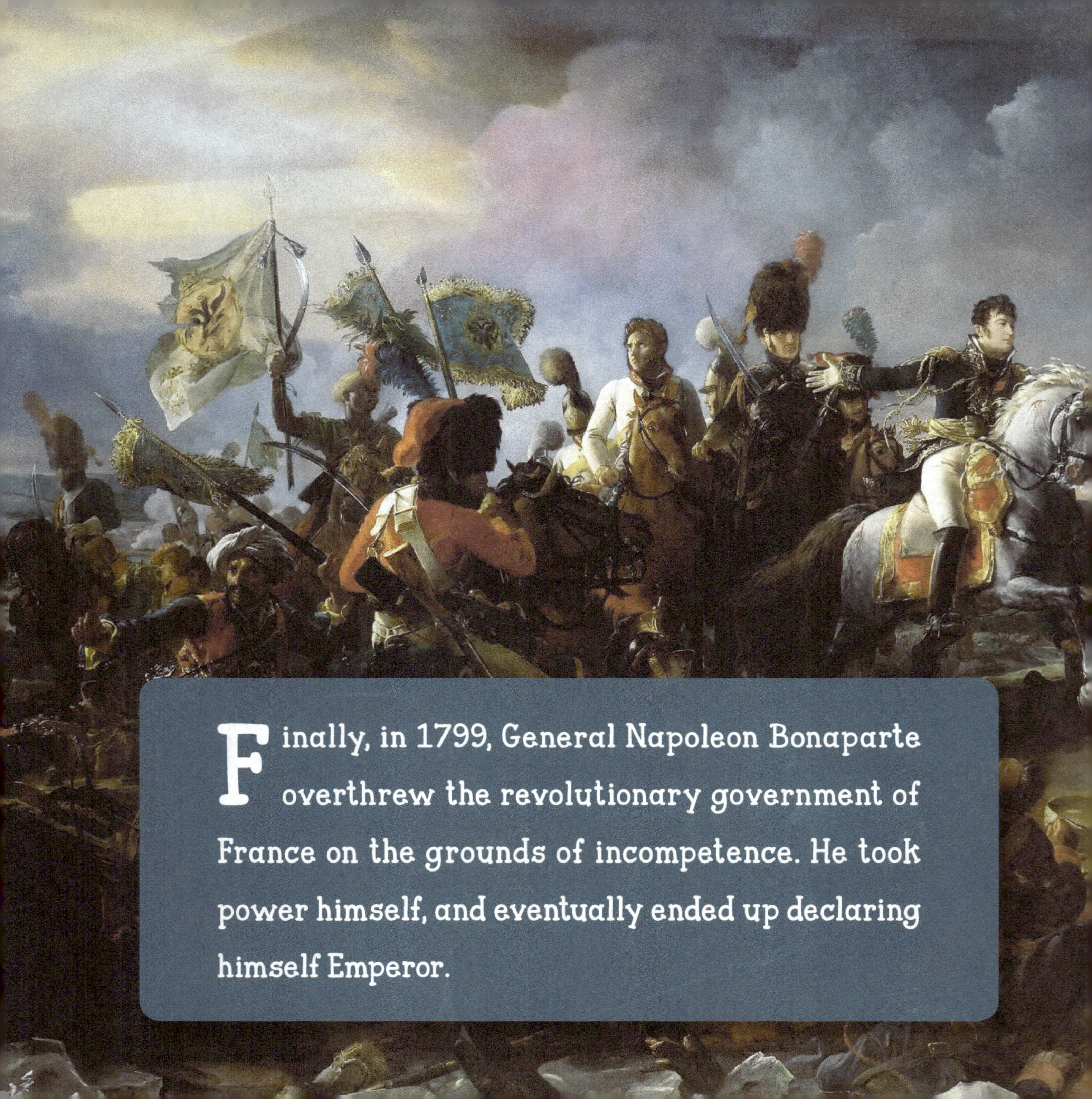

Finally, in 1799, General Napoleon Bonaparte overthrew the revolutionary government of France on the grounds of incompetence. He took power himself, and eventually ended up declaring himself Emperor.

NAPOLEON IN THE BATTLE OF AUSTERLITZ

FRENCH REVOLUTION

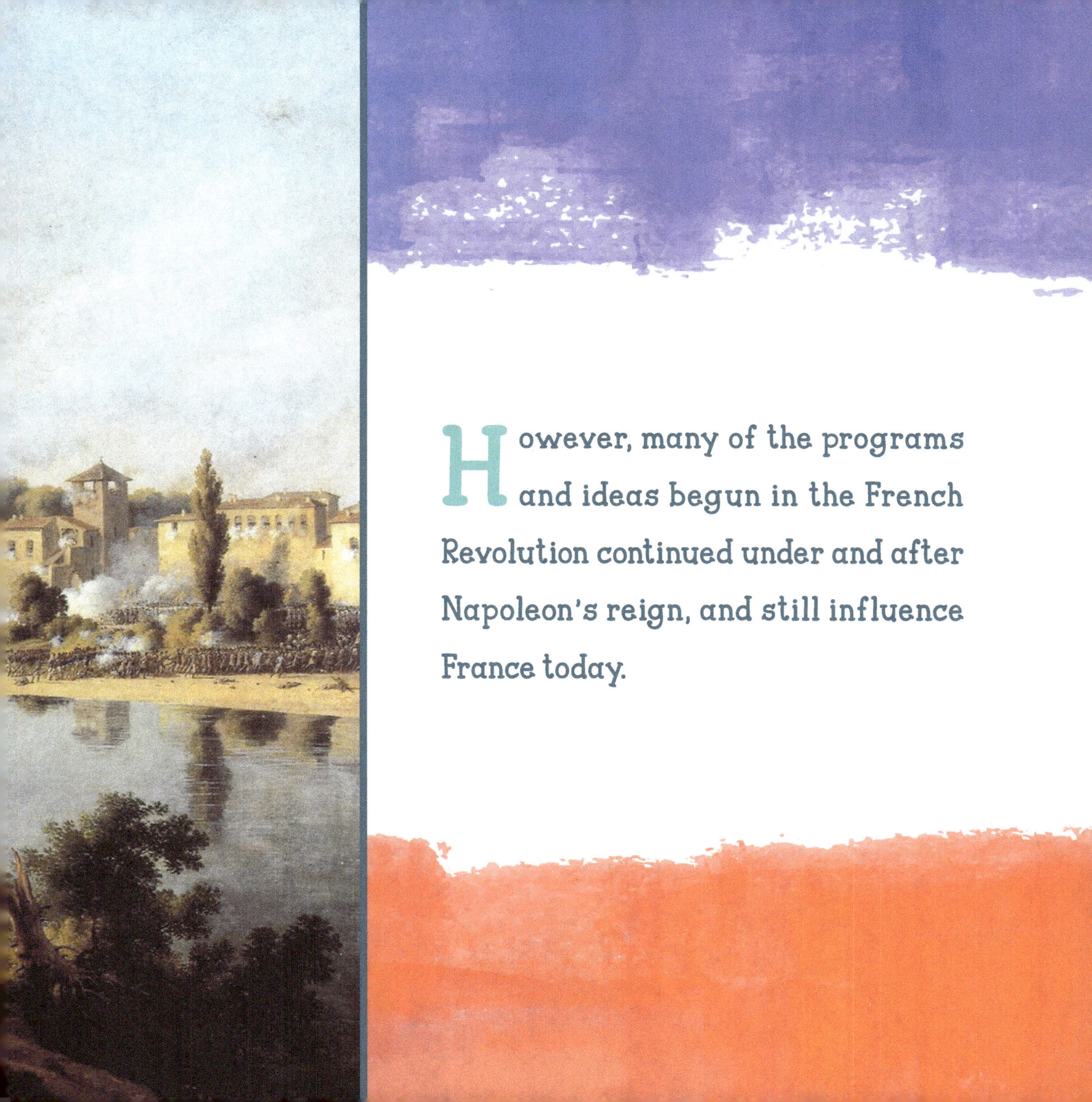

However, many of the programs and ideas begun in the French Revolution continued under and after Napoleon's reign, and still influence France today.

THE BEST OF TIMES, THE WORST OF TIMES

Charles Dickens' novel of the French Revolution, A Tale of Two Cities, begins, "It was the best of times, it was the worst of times…" From the grand dreams, violent horrors and great changes of the revolution emerged a different France from the country the kings had ruled.

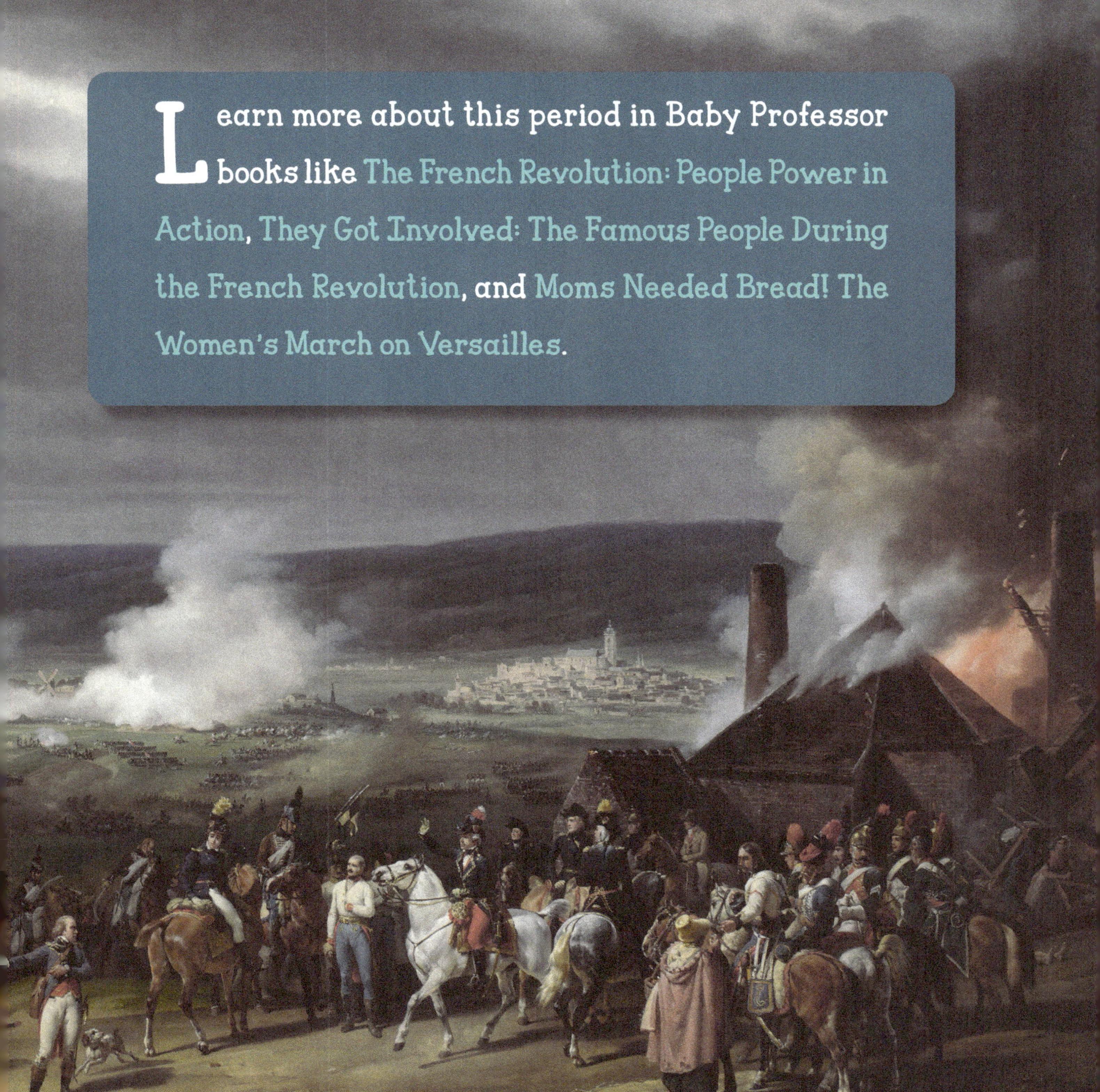

Learn more about this period in Baby Professor books like The French Revolution: People Power in Action, They Got Involved: The Famous People During the French Revolution, and Moms Needed Bread! The Women's March on Versailles.

Visit
BABY PROFESSOR
EDUCATION KIDS
www.BabyProfessorBooks.com
to download Free Baby Professor eBooks
and view our catalog of new and exciting
Children's Books